MARY HAD A CROCODILE

and other funny animal verse

Chosen by Jennifer Curry

Illustrated by Mark Burgess

Beaver Books

Also in Beaver by Jennifer Curry

The Beaver Book of Skool Verse
Treasure Trove

With Graeme Curry
The Beaver Book of Revolting Rhymes

A Beaver Book
Published by Arrow Books Limited
17–21 Conway Street, London W1P 6JD

An imprint of the Hutchinson Publishing Group

London Melbourne Sydney Auckland
Johannesburg and agencies throughout the world

First published 1985
This collection © Jennifer Curry 1985
Illustrations © the Hutchinson Publishing Group 1985

Set in Linoterm Bembo by
JH Graphics Limited, Reading, Berks

Made and printed in Great Britain
by Anchor Brendon Ltd
Tiptree, Essex

ISBN 0 09 938510 4

Contents

This book is dedicated, with my love and admiration, to the kids next door, T, D and T

All Things Bright
and Beautiful . . .

The Hairy Dog

My dog's so furry I've not seen
His face for years and years:
His eyes are buried out of sight,
I only guess his ears.

When people ask me for his breed,
I do not know or care:
He has the beauty of them all
Hidden beneath his hair.

Herbert Asquith

Tibetan Lament

The loveliest of our lamas
Is gone beyond the door.
He'll never wear pyjamas
Any more, any more.

Above the yawning chasm
He tried to pass a yak;
It took a sneezing spasm
And blew him off his track.
Now the silent valley has him,
And he can't come back.

The loveliest of our lamas
Is gone beyond the door.
He'll never wear pyjamas
Any more.

Anon

The Hen

No bird can sing so sweetly
        As the Hen;
No bird can walk so neatly,
        And again,
    Apart from being beautiful,
    I know no bird so dutiful,
For it lays an egg discreetly –
        Now and then.

How nice, when dawn is bringing
        In the day,
To wake and hear it singing
        O'er its *lay*.
    Ah yes! how good the Hen is,
    So save up all your pennies,
And buy one (one with trousers) –
        It will pay.

John Joy Bell

The Geese in Greece

The geese
in Greece
grow white
woolly fleece,
which is made
into shawls
in the Peloponnese.
Nice
heartwarming
geese.

N. M. Bodecker

A Song of Toad

The world has held great Heroes,
    As history-books have showed;
But never a name to go down to fame
    Compared to that of Toad!

The clever men at Oxford
    Know all that there is to be knowed.
But they none of them know one half as much
    As intelligent Mr Toad!

The animals sat in the ark and cried,
    Their tears in torrents flowed.
Who was it said, 'There's land ahead'?
    Encouraging Mr Toad!

The Army all saluted
  As they marched along the road.
Was it the King? Or Kitchener?
  No. It was Mr Toad.

The Queen and her ladies-in-waiting
  Sat at the window and sewed.
She cried, 'Look! who's that *handsome* man?'
  They answered, 'Mr Toad.'

The motor-car went Poop-poop-poop
  As it raced along the road.
Who was it steered it into a pond?
  Ingenious Mr Toad!

Kenneth Grahame

The Duck-billed Platypus

We call him 'Duck-billed Platypus'
And mock him for his name;
He does not seem to mind it.
He feels no sense of shame
Because he does not know himself
By such a title,
He's
A 'Golden, Shining Love-Bird'
In Duck-billed Platypese.

Michael Flanders

My Pony

Over the fields and far away,
My pony and I go out to play.
Elsa's a piebald, nearly six,
She's full of fun and rarely kicks.

She tosses her head and flicks her tail,
And eats her oats from a yellow pail.
She and I are such very good friends,
I hope this friendship never ends.

I love her and she loves me,
And we are one in harmony.
Over the fields and far away,
My pony and I go out to play.

Rachel Keefe (aged 9)

The Singing Cat

It was a little captive cat
Upon a crowded train
His mistress takes him from his box
To ease his fretful pain.

She holds him tight upon her knee
The graceful animal
And all the people look at him
He is so beautiful.

But oh he pricks and oh he prods
And turns upon her knee
Then lifteth up his innocent voice
In plaintive melody.

He lifteth up his innocent voice
He lifteth up, he singeth
And to each human countenance
A smile of grace he bringeth.

He lifteth up his innocent paw
Upon her breast he clingeth
And everybody cries, Behold
The cat, the cat that singeth.

He lifteth up his innocent voice
He lifteth up, he singeth
And all the people warm themselves
In the love his beauty bringeth.

Stevie Smith

This and That

Two cats together
In bee-heavy weather
After the August day
In smug contentment lay
By the garden shed
In the flower bed
Yawning out the hours
In the shade of the flowers
And passed the time away,
Between stretching and washing and sleeping,
Talking over the day.

'Climbed a tree.'
'Aaaah.'
'Terrorized sparrows.'
'Mmmmh.'
'Was chased.'
'Aaaah.'
'Fawned somewhat!'
'Mmmmh.'
'Washed, this and that.'
Said the first cat.

And they passed the time away
Between stretching and washing and sleeping
Talking over the day.

'Gazed out of parlour window.'
'Aaaah.'
'Pursued blue bottles.'
'Mmmmh.'
'Clawed curtains.'
'Aaaah.'
'Was cuffed.'
'Mmmmh.'
'Washed, this and that.'
Said the other cat.

And they passed the time away
Between stretching and washing and sleeping
Talking over the day.

'Scratched to be let in.'
'Aaaah.'
'Patrolled the house.'
'Mmmmh.'
'Scratched to go out.'
'Aaaah.'
'Was booted.'
'Mmmmh.'
'Washed, this and that.'
Said the first cat.

And they passed the time away
Between stretching and washing and sleeping
Talking over the day.

'Lapped cream elegantly.'
'Aaaah.'
'Disdained dinner.'
'Mmmmh.'
'Borrowed a little salmon.'
'Aaaah.'
'Was tormented.'
'Mmmmh.'
'Washed, this and that.'
Said the other cat.

And they passed the time away
Between stretching and washing and sleeping
Talking over the day.

Gareth Owen

Riddle

Riddle me, riddle me,
Riddle me ree,
I saw a nutcracker
Up in a tree.

Squirrel

The Cow

4 stiff-standers,
4 lily-landers,
2 lookers, 2 crookers,
And a wig-wag.

Anon

Chameleons

Chameleons are seldom seen,
They're red, they're orange, then they're green.
They're one of nature's strangest sights,
Their colours change like traffic lights.

Colin West

The Weasel

One morning a weasel came swimming
All the way over from France,
And taught all the weasels of England
To play on the fiddle and dance.

Anon

The Weasel

The Weasel is a perfect dear,
He'll never give you cause to fear.

If you walk out on a fine day,
He bounds before you all the way.

And if your boots are rather tight,
He bites them till they fit all right.

Lord Alfred Douglas

The Ferret

There is one animal of merit
And perfect honesty: the Ferret.

I have not time to tell to you
The numerous things that he will do.

For if you do not overtask him,
He will do anything you ask him.

He is as clever as a pike,
He will do anything you like.

He is as faithful as a bear,
And gentle as a Belgian hare.

He is as strong as any fish,
He will do anything you wish:

Bite holes in leaves, tie knots in string,
Or practically anything.

Lord Alfred Douglas

Grandpa Grig

Grandpa Grig had a pig
In a field of clover;
Piggie died, Grandpa cried,
And all the fun was over.

Anon

He Was a Rat

He was a rat, and she was a rat,
   And down in one hole they did dwell,
And both were as black as a witch's cat,
   And they loved each other well.

He had a tail, and she had a tail,
   Both long and curling and fine;
And each said, 'Yours is the finest tail
   In the world, excepting mine.'

He smelt the cheese, and she smelt the cheese,
   And they both pronounced it good;
And both remarked it would greatly add
   To the charms of their daily food.

So he ventured out, and she ventured out,
   And I saw them go with pain;
But what befell them I never can tell,
   For they never came back again.

Anon

Three Young Rats

Three young rats with black felt hats,
Three young ducks with white straw flats,
Three young dogs with curling tails,
Three young cats with demi-veils,

Went out to walk with three young pigs
In satin vests and sorrel wigs.
  But suddenly it chanced to rain
  And so they all went home again.

Anon

Pigs

Pigs are big and pink and round,
They sniff along the muddy ground,
And when they see a nice soft spot,
They jump in with a happy plop.

Katie Sandford (aged 9)

Hunc, Said He

There was a lady loved a swine.
'Honey,' said she,
'Pig-hog, wilt thou be mine?'
'Hunc,' said he.

'I'll build for thee a silver sty,
Honey,' said she,
'And in it softly thou shalt lie.'
'Hunc,' said he.

'Pinned with a silver pin,
Honey,' said she,
'That you may go both out and in.'
'Hunc,' said he.

'When shall we two be wed,
Honey?' said she.
'Hunc, hunc, hunc,' he said,
And away went he.

Anon

Seal

See how he dives
From the rocks with a zoom!
See how he darts
Through his watery room
Past crabs and eels
And green seaweed,
Past fluffs of sandy
Minnow feed!
See how he swims
With a swerve and a twist,
A flip of the flipper,
A flick of the wrist!
Quicksilver-quick,
Softer than spray,
Down he plunges
And sweeps away;
Before you can think,
Before you can utter
Words like 'Dill pickle'
Or 'Apple butter',
Back up he swims
Past sting-ray and shark,
Out with a zoom,
A whoom, a bark;
Before you can say
Whatever you wish,
He plops at your side
With a mouthful of fish!

William Jay Smith

All Creatures Great
and Small . . .

Mary Had a Crocodile

Mary had a crocodile
That ate a child each day;
But interfering people came
And took her pet away.

The Yak

As a friend to the children commend me the
    Yak.
   You will find it exactly the thing:
It will carry and fetch, you can ride on its back,
   Or lead it about with a string.

The Tartar who dwells on the plains of Tibet
   (A desolate region of snow)
Has for centuries made it a nursery pet,
   And surely the Tartar should know!

Then tell your papa where the Yak can be got,
   And if he is awfully rich
He will buy you the creature – or else he will
    not.
   (I cannot be positive which.)

Hilaire Belloc

The Whale

There was a most Monstrous Whale:
He had no Skin, he had no Tail.
When he tried to Spout, that great Big Lubber,
The best he could do was Jiggle his Blubber.

Theodore Roethke

The Panther

The panther is like a leopard,
Except it hasn't been peppered.
Should you behold a panther crouch,
Prepare to say Ouch.
Better yet, if called by a panther,
Don't anther.

Ogden Nash

Radi

Radi was a circus lion,
Radi was a woman hater.
Radi had a lady trainer,
Radiator.

Anon

The Lion

The Lion is an awful bore,
He comes and dabbles in your gore.

And if he wants to have a feed,
He bites your leg and makes it bleed.

Although the tears stream from your eyes,
He takes no notice of your cries.

In vain you argue or protest,
He finishes his meal with zest.

Nor will he take the least rebuff
Until he feels he's had enough.

Lord Alfred Douglas

Mr Giraffe

O Mister Giraffe, you make me laugh,
You seem to be made all wrong;
Your head is so high up there in the sky
And your neck is so very long
That your dinner and tea, it seems to me,
Have such a long way to go,
And I'm wondering how they manage to know
The way to your tummy below.

Geoffrey Lapage

Excess of Elephants

The Eccentric Elephant

There was an elephant at the zoo,
Who,
Said he was born in Timbuctoo.

There was an elephant at the zoo,
Who,
Stuck his tail on with superglue.

There was an elephant at the zoo,
Who,
Solved the problem of two times two.

There was an elephant at the zoo,
Who,
Liked his cage bars painted bright blue.

There was an elephant at the zoo,
Who,
On his foreleg had a tattoo.

There was an elephant at the zoo,
Who,
Each day for dinner ate beef stew.

There was an elephant at the zoo,
Who,
Mastered the way to use the loo.

There was an elephant at the zoo,
Who,
From the spectators caught the flu.

There was an elephant at the zoo,
Who,
Only lived until he was two.

There was an elephant at the zoo,
Who,
I wish I had met, don't you?

Helen Boddy (aged 12)

The Elephant

When people bear this beast to mind,
They marvel more and more
At such a LITTLE tail behind,
So LARGE a trunk before.

Hilaire Belloc

Elephant

It is quite unfair to be
obliged to be so large, so I suppose
you could call me discontented.

Think big, they said, when
I was a little elephant; they
wanted to get me used to it.

It was kind. But it doesn't help if,
inside, you are carefree in small ways,
fond of little amusements.

You are smaller than me, think
how conveniently near the flowers are,
how you can pat the cat by just

halfbending over. You can also
arrange teacups for dolls, play
marbles in the proper season.

I would give anything to be
able to do a tiny, airy, flitting
dance to show how very little a

thing happiness can be really.

Alan Brownjohn

Eletelephony

Once there was an elephant,
Who tried to use the telephant –
No! no! I mean an elephone
Who tried to use the telephone –
(Dear me! I am not certain quite
That even now I've got it right.)

Howe'er it was, he got his trunk
Entangled in the telephunk;
The more he tried to get it free,
The louder buzzed the telephee –
(I fear I'd better drop the song
Of elephop and telephong!)

Laura E. Richards

Elephant in a Rhubarb Tree

Ha ha ha! He he he!
Elephant in a rhubarb tree,
Elephant said to the flea, 'Don't push,
Plenty of room in the next door bush.'

Anon

The Infant Elephant Speaks:

I got a rusk
stuck on my tusk

Adrian Mitchell

Riddle

He travels so much,
And wherever he goes,
He carries his trunk
At the end of his nose.

Anon

Gorilla

A giant Gorilla came to tea,
Whoever asked him? It wasn't me.
He came in through the kitchen wall,
It took six chairs to seat him all.
He drank his tea straight from the pot,
And sandwiches – he ate the lot.
He poked the jellies to make them wobble,
Then swallowed them up with just one gobble.
All that remained on the plate was the cake,
There was nothing else for him to take.
When he'd eaten that I showed him the door,
And hoped he'd go now there was no more.
Instead he ate the door as well,
Except for the knocker and the bell.
After that he at last decided to go,
Who invited him? I'd like to know.

Martin Honeysett

The Walrus

The Walrus lives on icy floes
And unsuspecting Eskimoes.

Don't bring your wife to Arctic Tundra
A Walrus may bob up from undra.

Michael Flanders

The Truth about
the Abominable Footprint

The Yeti's a Beast
Who lives in the East
   And suffers a lot from B.O.
His hot hairy feet
Stink out the street
   So he cools them off in the snow.

Michael Baldwin

Anaconda

A snake to fear
Is the anaconda,
He stretches from here

                              to over yonder.

Doug Macleod

The Crocodile's Toothache

The Crocodile
Went to the dentist
And sat down in the chair,
And the dentist said, 'Now tell me, sir,
Why does it hurt and where?'
And the Crocodile said, 'I'll tell you the truth,
I have a terrible ache in my tooth,'
And he opened his jaws so wide, so wide,
That the dentist, he climbed right inside,
And the dentist laughed, 'Oh isn't this fun?'
As he pulled the teeth out, one by one.
And the Crocodile cried, 'You're hurting me so!
Please put down your pliers and let me go.'
But the dentist just laughed with a Ho Ho Ho,
And he said, 'I still have twelve to go –
Oops, that's the wrong one, I confess,
But what's one crocodile's tooth, more or less?'
Then suddenly, the jaws went SNAP,
And the dentist was gone, right off the map,
And where he went one could only guess . . .
To North or South or East or West . . .
He left no forwarding address.
But what's one dentist, more or less?

Shel Silverstein

Big Aunt Flo

Every Sunday afternoon
She visits us for tea
And weighs–in somewhere between
A rhino and a flea.
    (But closer to the rhino!)

Aunt Flo tucks into doughnuts,
Eats fruit cake by the tin.
Her stomach makes strange noises
Just like my rude friend, Flynn.
    (Sounds more like a goat, really!)

Then after tea she heads for
The best chair in the room
And crashes on the cushions
With one resounding boom.
    (You'd think a door had slammed!)

Flo sits on knitting needles
And snaps them with a crack.
She squashes dolls and jigsaws
Behind her massive back.
    (And she doesn't feel a thing!)

But Aunt Flo learned a lesson,
There's no doubt about that,
Last Sunday when she grabbed the chair
And sat down on our cat.
    (Big Tom, a cat with a temper!)

The beast let out a wild yell
And dug his claws in . . . deep.
Poor Flo clutched her huge behind
And gave a mighty leap.
   (She almost reached the ceiling!)

So now at Sunday teatime
Jam doughnuts going spare.
Dad winks, and asks where Flo is.
While Tom sleeps on *that* chair.
   (And he's purring, the devil!)

Wes Magee

To the Bat

Bat, bat, come under my hat,
   And I'll give you a slice of bacon;
And when I bake, I'll give you a cake,
   If I am not mistaken.

Anon

Who's That Ringing at My Door Bell?

Who's that ringing at my door bell?
   A little pussy cat that isn't very well.
Rub its little nose with a little mutton fat,
   For that's the best cure for a little pussy cat.

Anon

Busy Little Beaver

I'm a busy little Beaver,
I make things out of logs,
Not only dams but other things,
Like fencing posts and clogs.
I can gnaw you up
Some garden gates,
Or shelves on which
To stack your plates,
And if trade gets
A little poor,
I sell clothes pegs
From door to door.
But because I've been so busy,
I've worn out all my teeth,
And I haven't any more,
Growing up from underneath.
I tried to work without them,
But it made my gums so raw,
That now I do my woodwork,
With a little power saw.

Martin Honeysett

A Pig Tale

Two little pigs to market went,
    Their names were Paul and Patience.
They both were sold and both were sent
    To different destinations.

And as the pair were dragged apart
   Paul said in soothing tones:
'Don't cry, we'll meet again, sweetheart;
   I feel it in my bones.'

    ★   ★   ★

They did meet at an early date;
   He had not been mistaken,
Paul was the sausage on my plate
   And Patience was the bacon.

Anon

Cheetie–Poussie–Cattie, O

There was a wee bit mousikie,
That leeved in Gilberaty, O;
It couldna get a bit o cheese,
For Cheetie–Poussie–Cattie, O.

It said unto the cheesikie,
'O fain wad I be at ye, O,
If it werena for the cruel paws
O' Cheetie–Poussie–Cattie, O.'

Anon

Beg Parding

'Beg parding, Mrs Harding,
Is my kitting in your garding?'

'Is your kitting in my garding?
Yes she is, and all alone,
Chewing of a mutting bone.'

Anon

Lost Chickens

My chickens lay eggs like bananas,
they're bendy and yellow and sweet
and the man round the corner has told me
his garden grows mushrooms with feet.

My favourite dinner was omelette
eaten outdoors with a spoon.
The fork is for mashing the mushrooms
when they run to the feast of the moon.

We shall dance round the fire of an evening,
holding hands as we sing an old song,
'Oh Moon, shine on every lost chicken!'
The new omelettes keep on going wrong.

Jane Whittle

Wouldn't Lay an Egg

Had a little chicky,
It wouldn't lay an egg.
Poured hot water
Up and down its leg.

Little chicky cried,
Little chicky begged,
Little chicky laid
A hard-boiled egg.

Anon

Old Shellover

'Come!' said Old Shellover.
'What?' says Creep.
'The horny old Gardener's fast asleep;
The fat cock Thrush
To his nest has gone;
And the dew shines bright
In the rising Moon;
Old Sallie Worm from her hole doth peep:
Come!' said Old Shellover.
'Ay!' said Creep.

Walter de la Mare

Hannibal the Snail

Along the playground tarmac
Signing it with his trail,
Glides Hannibal the Hero
Hannibal the snail.

Under the burning sun
In the asphalt desert dust,
Hannibal with a placard
'TO THE FOOTBALL FIELD OR BUST!'

Spurning food or drink,
Refusing offers of aid,
Hannibal hurries slowly on
And won't be put in the shade.

His trail is snail miles long
Its silver is tarnished and dimming
But Hannibal shoulders his dusty shell
And points his horns to winning.

Triumphant he glides to the balm of the grass,
Into the cool of the clover,
Hannibal's crossed his desert
His impossible journey is over.

He slides through the dandelions
Exploring each stalk and stem byway
And could that be Hannibal singing
'I did it my way'?

Julie Holder

Heaps of Hippos

Hippopotamuses

Hippopotamuses never
Put on boots in rainy weather.
To slosh in mud up to their ears
Brings them great joy and merry tears.
Their pleasure lies in being messed up
They just won't play at being dressed up.
In fact a swamp is heaven plus
If you're a hippopotamus.

Arnold Spilka

The Hippopotamus

The huge hippopotamus hasn't a hair
on the back of his wrinkly hide;
he carries the bulk of his prominent hulk
rather loosely assembled inside.

The huge hippopotamus lives without care
at a slow philosophical pace,
as he wades in the mud with a thump and a thud
and a permanent grin on his face.

Jack Prelutsky

Hippoportant Poem . . .

A hippopotamus
Would squash a lot of us
If it sat on us.

Mike Harding

The Habits of the Hippopotamus

The hippopotamus is strong
   And huge of head and broad of bustle;
The limbs on which he rolls along
   Are big with hippopotomuscle.

He does not greatly care for sweets
   Like ice cream, apple pie or custard,
But takes to flavour what he eats
   A little hippopotomustard.

The hippopotamus is true
   To all his principles, and just;
He always tries his best to do
   The things one hippopotomust.

He never rides in trucks or trams,
   In taxicabs or omnibuses,
And so keeps out of traffic jams
   And other hippopotomusses.

Arthur Guiterman

Consider the Poor Hippopotamus!

Consider the poor hippopotamus:
His life is unduly monotonous.
He lives half asleep
At the edge of the deep,
And his face is as big as his bottom is.

Anon

Mosquito

At night
when I'm tucked tight in bed
you whine and dive
around my head.
You walk
   and stalk me
     up the sheet
with stick legs
bent up into feet.
There isn't any way you please
with elbows
where you should have knees –
and here's another horrid thing –
   you've got a sting.

Peggy Dunstan

There Once Was a Boy

There once was a boy of Bagdad.
An inquisitive sort of a lad.
    He said, 'I will see
    If a sting has a bee.'
And he very soon found that it had.

Anon

The Cure

'I've swallowed a fly,' cried Marjorie Fry.
   (We could hear it buzzing inside her.)
'And I haven't a hope of getting it out
   Unless I swallow a spider.'

We found a web by the garden wall,
   And back to the house we hurried
And offered the spider to Marjorie Fry,
   Who was looking extremely worried.

'Now shut your eyelids, Marjorie Fry,
   And open your wee mouth wider.
Whatever it does, the fly won't buzz
   If only you'll swallow the spider.'

Alfred Noyes

There Was an Old Person

There was an old person of Skye,
Who waltzed with a bluebottle fly;
   They buzzed a sweet tune,
   To the light of the moon,
And entranced all the people of Skye.

Edward Lear

In Hall

'All things bright and beautiful . . .'
How many late today?
There's mud all up the front staircase,
What is she going to say?

It's hot in here, I'm going to sneeze.
'All creatures great and small . . .'
A spider's dangling over her!
Where is it going to fall?

It might land softly in her hair –
would she feel it, d'you suppose?
Or, if it swung a little bit,
it might settle on her nose.

'All things wise and wonderful . . .'
The teachers stand in line.
It's only got an inch to go!
This may be a sign.

Oh, land on her, please land on her!
'The Lord God made them all . . .'
Then she'll forget she saw me there –
I was here, in Hall,

I wasn't late, I didn't leave
my footsteps on the stairs . . .
Oh! Spider, you must hurry up,
she's halfway through the prayers.

Spider, spider, burning bright . . .
'Three girls I want to see.
Where are you? You, and you, and . . . Oh!
What's this? Oh dear! Dear me! . . .'

A hundred eyes, eight hairy legs,
A shadow on the wall.
I wasn't there, I wasn't late.
The Lord God loves us all!

Jane Whittle

Morning

The flower heads hang heavily
As the bee swims inside.
Sun has just risen,
Night has just died;
Outside in the garden,
An awful sound is heard,
An early worm is eaten,
By an early bird.

Stuart Bage (aged 11)

A Spider for Luck

If you want to live and thrive
Let a spider run alive.

Playground chant

Christmas Dinner

We were all sitting round the table.
There was roast turkey
there were roast potatoes
there were roast parsnips
there were broccoli tips
there was a dishful of crispy bacon off the
    turkey
there was wine, cider, beer, lemonade
and milk – for the youngsters.
Everything was set.
It was all on the table.
We were ready to begin.
Suddenly there was a terrible terrible scream.
Right next to the turkey was a worm.
A dirty little worm wriggling about like mad.

For a moment everyone looked at it.
Someone said very quietly, 'Oh dear.'
And everyone was thinking things like –
'How did it get there?'
'If that came out of the turkey,
I don't want any of it.'
or
'I'm not eating any Christmas dinner. It could
    be full of
dirty little wriggly worms.'

Now – as it happens,
I don't mind wriggly worms.
There was plenty of room for it
at the table.
It was just that . . . that . . .
no-one had asked it to come over
for Christmas dinner.

So I said,
'I don't think it came out of the turkey. I think –
It came off the bottom of the milk bottle.'
And I picked up the worm,
and put it out the door to spend Christmas day
in a lovely patch of wet mud.
Much nicer place to be –
for a worm.

Michael Rosen

Cyril the Centipede

Cyril the centipede
Loved playing games,
And his favourite one was football.
And when he played goal
With nine fleas and a mole
Nothing got past him at all.

They played spiders and newts
But his one hundred boots
Gave his team very little to do
And the fleas would get bored,
And the mole never scored
And the crowd would just stand there and boo.

Till one awful day the crowd stayed away
And no fans for either side came,
But all said and done
When it's none none none none,
It's not really much of a game.
Then Cyril the centipede
Hurt his back leg
The hundredth one down on the right
So he used a small stick
And went 99 click,
Now I'm happy to say it's all right.

But he doesn't play goal
Any more – he's retired
Unbeaten, for nobody scored.
Now he just referees
For the spiders and fleas,
And even the mole
Has just scored.

Jeremy Lloyd

He Stood on the Bridge

He stood on the bridge at midnight,
Disturbing my sweet repose,
For he was a large mosquito –
And the bridge was the bridge of my nose.

Anon

A Bug and a Flea

A bug and a flea
Went out to sea
Upon a reel of cotton;
The flea was drowned
But the bug was found
Biting a lady's bottom.

Playground song

House Flies

What makes
common house flies
trying
is
that they keep
multiflieing.

N. M. Bodecker

My Obnoxious Brother Bobby

My obnoxious brother Bobby
Has a most revolting hobby;
There, behind the garden wall is
Where he captures creepy-crawlies.

Grannies, aunts and baby cousins
Come to our house in their dozens,
But they disappear discreetly
When they see him smiling sweetly.

For they know, as he approaches,
In his pockets are cockroaches,
Spiders, centipedes and suchlike;
All of which they do not much like.

As they head towards the lobby,
Bidding fond farewells to Bobby,
How they wish he'd change his habits
And keep guinea pigs or rabbits.

But their wishes are quite futile,
For he thinks that bugs are cute. I'll
Finish now, but just remind you:
Bobby could be right behind you!

Colin West

All Things Wise
and Wonderful . . .

Three Owls in a Wood

There once were three owls in a wood
Who always sang hymns when they could:
What the words were about
One could never make out,
But one felt it was doing them good.

Anon

My Grandpa

The truth of the matter, the truth of the matter –
As one who supplies us with hats is a Hatter,
As one who is known for his growls is a
    Growler –
My grandpa traps owls, yes, my grandpa's an
    Owler.

Though owls, alas, are quite out of fashion,
Grandpa keeps busy about his profession
And hoards every owl that falls to his traps:
'Someday,' says he, 'they'll be needed, perhaps.'

'Owls are such sages,' he says, 'I surmise
Listening to owls could make the world wise.'
Nightlong his house is shaken with hoots,
And he wakes to owls in his socks and his
    boots.

Owls, owls, nothing but owls,
The most fantastical of fowls:
White owls from the Arctic, black owls from
  the Tropic.
Some are far-sighted, others myopic.

There are owls on his picture frames, owls on
  his chairs,
Owls in dozens ranked on his stairs.
Eyes, eyes, rows of their eyes,
Some are big as collie dogs, some are
  thumb-size.

Deep into Africa, high into Tibet
He travels with his rubber mouse and wiry
  owl-net:
The rarest of owls, and the very most
  suspicious
Will pounce on the mouse and be tangled in the
  meshes.

'Whatever you could wish to know, an owl will
  surely know it,'
My grandpa says proudly. 'And how does he
  show it?
Sleeping and thinking and sleeping and
  thinking –
Letting a horrible hoot out and winking!'

Ted Hughes

Wise Old Owl

A wise old owl sat in an oak,
The more he heard, the less he spoke;
The less he spoke, the more he heard,
Why aren't we all like that wise old bird?

Anon

The Sloth

In moving-slow he has no Peer,
You ask him something in his ear,
He thinks about it for a year;

And, then, before he says a Word
There, upside down (unlike a Bird),
He will assume that you have Heard —

A most Ex-as-per-at-ing Lug.
But should you call his manner Smug,
He'll sigh and give his Branch a Hug;

Then off again to Sleep he goes,
Still swaying gently by his Toes,
And you just know he knows he knows.

Theodore Roethke

Parrot

Sometimes I sit with both eyes closed,
But all the same, I've heard!
They're saying, 'He won't talk because
He is a *thinking* bird.'

I'm olive-green and sulky, and
The family say, 'Oh yes,
He's silent, but he's *listening*,
He *thinks* more than he *says*!

'He ponders on the things he hears,
Preferring not to chatter.'
– And this is true, but *why* it's true
Is quite another matter.

I'm working out some shocking things
In order to surprise them,
And when my thoughts are ready I'll
Certainly *not* disguise them!

I'll wait, and see, and choose a time
When everyone is present,
And clear my throat and raise my beak
And give a squawk and start to speak
And go on for about a week
And it will not be pleasant!

Alan Brownjohn

Sergeant Brown's Parrot and Sir Robert Mark

Sir Robert Mark, Police Commissioner,
Heard of a Sergeant who had dared to position a

Parrot on his shoulder. 'A what?' he said.
'PARROT, TALL. GREEN. ALONGSIDE
  HIS HEAD.

SMART. WELL-SPOKEN. A BIRD OF
  BREEDING.
PROCEEDS WHEREVER THE
  SERGEANT'S PROCEEDING.'

The report was delivered at a Working
  Luncheon.
Sir Robert banged his plate with his silver
  truncheon.

The plate broke in half. No–one dared to laugh.
'Bring this man in!' he roared to his staff.

The Sergeant was working on a dog theft case,
Sitting at his desk with his parrot in place.

'Come on, Brown!' they yelled, 'better make it
  snappy –
Sir Robert Mark wants you and he isn't too
  happy!'

So off went the Sergeant and the parrot and the
   rest of them,
Arrived where Sir Robert was scoffing with the
   best of them.

Sergeant and parrot strolled into the meeting.
Everyone stopped talking. Everyone stopped
   eating.

Sir Robert looked the pair of them up and down
With a dangerous look in his eye. He said:
   'Brown,

I've seen some things in the Force, my *word*
   upon it,
But never once a Sergeant with a shoulder with
   a bird upon it.

Take it off at once, you ridiculous clown!'
'Shut your beak,' said Sergeant Brown.

                                        Kit Wright

Mr Fox

Dear old Mr Fox,
He needs a Christmas box,
A hat and a coat
And a pair of khaki socks.

Playground rhyme

The Three Foxes

Once upon a time there were three little foxes
Who didn't wear stockings, and they didn't
    wear sockses,
But they all had handkerchiefs to blow their
    noses,
And they kept their handkerchiefs in cardboard
    boxes.

They lived in the forest in three little houses,
And they didn't wear coats, and they didn't
    wear trousies.
They ran through the woods on their little bare
    tootsies,
And they played 'Touch last' with a family of
    mouses.

They didn't go shopping in the High Street
    shopses,
But caught what they wanted in the woods and
    copses.
They all went fishing, and they caught three
    wormses,
They went out hunting, and they caught three
    wopses.

They went to a Fair, and they all won prizes –
Three plum puddingses and three mince-
    pieses.
They rode on elephants and swang on
    swingses,
And hit three coco–nuts at coco–nut shieses.

That's all that I know of the three little foxes
Who kept their handkerchiefs in cardboard
    boxes.
They lived in the forest in three little houses,
But they didn't wear coats and they didn't wear
    trousies,
And they didn't wear stockings and they didn't
    wear sockses.

A. A. Milne

Wonderful Bird

A wonderful bird is the sea gull,
It can fly quite as high as an eagle.
    It will sit on the sand,
    And sometimes will stand,
But you can't tell a he from a she gull.

Anon

The Nonny

The Nonny-bird I love particularly;
    All day she chirps her joysome odes.
She rises perpendicularly,
    And if she goes too far, explodes.

James Reeves

The Great Auk's Ghost

The Great Auk's ghost rose on one leg,
Sighed thrice and three times winkt,
And turned and poached a phantom egg
And muttered, 'I'm extinct.'

Ralph Hodgson

Norman the Zebra

Norman, a zebra at the zoo,
Escaped and ran to Waterloo
And caused a lot of consternation
In the rush-hour, at the station.
He had an awful lot of fun
Chasing folk on Platform 1,
And then he ran to Regent's Park
And hid there until it was dark,
And thought of his keeper Mr Prout,
How cross he'd be, that he'd got out.
So he tiptoed to the big zoo gate
And found he'd got there just too late.
Poor Norman had a little weep
And lay down in the road to sleep
And woke up early from his rest,
With people walking on his chest.
And someone said, 'I think that's new,
A zebra crossing near the zoo.'
And with a snort of indignation,
Regretting leaving for the station,
He cried, 'I've had enough of that,
How dare you use me as a mat.
I'm going straight home to the zoo.'
He was just in time for breakfast too.

Jeremy Lloyd

Sid the Rat

Sid was a rat
Who kept a hat shop,
Ordinary sort of stuff:

Pork pies,
Panamas,
Old flat caps,
Bowlers,
Boaters
For old fat chaps,
Deerstalkers,
Stetsons . . .
And that was *enough*
For *that* shop!

Yes, Sid was a rat
Who kept a hat shop,
Ordinary sort of trade:

Eels,
Elks,
Dirty old foxes,
Skinny
Kittens
In travelling boxes,
Elephants,
Owls . . .
And business *paid*
In *that* shop!

One day the Mayor knocked on the door,
Said, 'Sid, you can't stay here no more!
We're going to knock your hat shop down
To build a new road through the town!'

'Is that a fact?'
Said Sid the Rat,
'Is that a fact?'
Said he.
'We'll see!

You build your road and I'll get my hats
And I'll stack them up like a block of flats
Right in the middle
And hey–diddle–diddle!
The cars won't know
Which way to go!
And I'll get the elk
And the dirty old fox
And the kitten
Out of her travelling box
And the slithering eel
And the wise owl too
And the elephant
On his way to the zoo
And I'll tell you what they'll do!

They'll pull those drivers out
Willy-nilly
And they'll tickle those drivers
And tickle them silly!
There'll be *huge* traffic jams
But they won't care!
So how do you like THAT,
Mr Mayor?'

'Oh,' said the Mayor.
'Oh dear,' said the Mayor.
'Hum,' said the Mayor.
'I fear,' said the Mayor,

You'd better keep your hat shop, Sid,
And carry on the way you did!'

Sid

Did!

Eleanor Oliphant

Jingle

Hoddley, poddley, puddle and fogs,
Cats are to marry the poodle dogs;
Cats in blue jackets and dogs in red hats,
What will become of the mice and the rats?

Anon

Bagpipes

Puss came dancing out of a barn
With a pair of bagpipes under her arm;
She could sing nothing but, Fiddle cum fee,
The mouse has married the humble-bee.
Pipe, cat – dance, mouse –
We'll have a wedding at our good house.

Anon

The Horny-Goloch

The horny-goloch is an awesome beast,
Soople an scaly;
It has twa horns, an a hantle o feet,
An a forkie tailie.

Anon

I'm Thor!

The thunder god went for a ride
Upon his favourite filly.
    'I'm Thor,' he cried,
    And the horse replied,
'You forgot your thaddle, thilly.'

Anon

Jocelyn, My Dragon

My dragon's name is Jocelyn,
He's something of a joke.
For Jocelyn is very tame,
He doesn't like to maul or maim,
Or breathe a fearsome fiery flame;
He's much too smart to smoke.

And when I take him to the park
The children form a queue,
And say, 'What lovely eyes of red!'
As one by one they pat his head.
And Jocelyn is so well-bred,
He only eats a few!

Colin West

Little Hairy Monster

A little hairy monster
Came crawling up to me
He looked so sad and lonely
I asked him up to tea
If only I had known
The fate that waited me
I'm down inside his stomach
As his favourite recipe.

Laura Milligan

The Blob

And . . . and what is it like?
        Oh, it's scary and fatbumped
        and spike–eared and groany.
        It's hairy and face–splumped
        and bolshie and bony.

And . . . and where does it live?
        Oh, in comets and spaceships
        and pulsars and blackholes.
        In craters and sheepdips
        and caverns and northpoles.

And . . . and what does it eat?
        Oh, roast rocks and fishlegs
        and x-rays and mooncrust.
        Then steelmeat and sun–eggs
        and lava and spacedust.

And . . . and who are its enemies?
        Oh, Zonkers and Moonquakes
        and Suquarks and Zigbags.
        Dumb Duncers and Milkshakes
        and Smogsters and Wigwags.

And . . . and what does it wear?
        Not a thing! It's bare!

Wes Magee

The Bogus-Boo

The Bogus-boo
Is a creature who
Comes out at night – and why?
He likes the air;
He likes to scare
The nervous passer-by.

Out from the park
At dead of dark
He comes with huffling pad
If, when alone,
You hear his moan,
'Tis like to drive you mad.

He has two wings,
Pathetic things,
With which he cannot fly.
His tusks look fierce,
Yet could not pierce
The merest butterfly.

He has six ears,
But what he hears
Is very faint and small;
And with the claws
On his eight paws
He cannot scratch at all.

He looks so wise
With his owl–eyes,
His aspect grim and ghoulish;
But truth to tell,
He sees not well
And is distinctly foolish.

The Bogus–boo,
What can he do
But huffle in the dark?
So don't take fright;
He has no bite
And very little bark.

James Reeves

Horse

The picnickers were sleeping when I,
deciding to be an enormous black horse not
    seen
in the corner of their field, strolled over.

They had a tartan rug, and a
thermos flask, and they had unwrapped
and eaten little triangles of processed

cheese, with tomatoes. They had been
playing cards among the thistles and
water-biscuits, and had fallen asleep

in the very hot sun. So I was a sudden, black
alarming shadow standing over them, though
    really
just inquisitive. When one of them heard the
    sound of my breath,

and woke, having dreamt of dragons, and
leapt up and shouted, *I* had to pretend to
be frightened of *them* and gallop away.

Alan Brownjohn

The Frog's Lament

'I can't bite
like a dog,'
said the bright
green frog.

'I can't nip,
I can't squirt,
I can't grip,
I can't hurt.

All I can do
is hop and hide
when enemies come
from far and wide.

I can't scratch
like a cat.
I'm no match
for a rat.

I can't stab,
I can't shove,
I can't grab,
I can't scare.

All I can do
my whole life through
is hop,' said the frog,
'and hide from view.'

And that's
what I saw him
up and do.

Aileen Fisher

The Triantiwontigongolope

There's a very funny insect that you do not
    often spy,
And it isn't quite a spider, and it isn't quite a fly;
It is something like a beetle, and a little like a
    bee,
But nothing like a woolly grub that climbs
    upon a tree.
Its name is quite a hard one, but you'll learn it
    soon, I hope,
So, try:
      Tri—
           Tri—anti—wonti—
             Triantiwontigongolope.

It lives on weeds and wattle-gum, and has a
    funny face;
Its appetite is hearty, and its manners a disgrace.
When first you come upon it, it will give you
    quite a scare,
But when you look for it again you find it isn't
    there.
And unless you call it softly it will stay away
    and mope.
So, try:
      Tri—
      Tri—anti—wonti—
             Triantiwontigongolope.

It trembles if you tickle it or tread upon its toes;
It is not an early riser, but it has a snubbish nose.
If you sneer at it, or scold it, it will scuttle off in
    shame,
But it purrs and purrs quite proudly if you call it
    by its name,
And offer it some sandwiches of sealing-wax
    and soap.
So, try:
        Tri–
        Tri–anti–wonti–
            Triantiwontigongolope.

But of course you haven't seen it; and I
    truthfully confess
That I haven't seen it either, and I don't know
    its address.
For there isn't such an insect, though there
    really might have been
If the trees and grass were purple, and the sky
    was bottle-green.
It's just a little joke of mine, which you'll
    forgive, I hope.
Oh, try:
        Try!
        Tri–anti–wonti–
            Triantiwontigongolope.

C. J. Dennis

Mohair
(The hair of an Angora goat)

Said the Angora goat
On a defensive note:
'It's better to have mohair
Than no hair.'

Roger Eckersley

Snowblind

Articfox
Was it,
Making trax
In the snow?
Or did my ice
Play trix?

Geoffrey Summerfield

There Once Was a Man

There once was a man who said, 'How
Shall I manage to carry my cow?
    For if I should ask it
    To get in my basket,
'T would make such a terrible row.'

Anon

Fuzzy Wuzzy

Fuzzy Wuzzy wuz a bear.
Fuzzy Wuzzy had no hair.
Fuzzy Wuzzy wuzn't fuzzy,
– Wuz he?

Anon

The Polar Bear

A polar bear who could not spell
Sat worrying in the snow.
'I wish,' he said, 'that I could tell
If *flow* is right, or *floe*.'
But as he worried up there came
A hungry Eskimo
Who shot him and – it seems a shame –
That bear will never knoe.

Edward Lucie-Smith

Riddle

Round the rocks
And round the rocks
The ragged rascal ran,
And every bush he came to,
He left his rags and ran.

Sheep

A Dog Is Loved

A dog is loved
    By old and young.
He wags his tail
    And not his tongue.

Anon

I Hate Dogs

Dirty dogs,
Smelly dogs,
Dirtying-the-pavement dogs,
Wretched, filthy, foul dogs –
Those are just a few.

Baby dogs,
Toy dogs,
Old, tatty, wild dogs,
Fierce-looking, wolf-like dogs –
Young dogs too.

Small dogs,
Black dogs,
Don't forget big dogs,
Last of all, stuffed dogs,
I like those best, don't you?

Simon A. Smith (aged 7)

Bear

There was a boy
who almost saw
a bear beside
his bed.

O bear, what are
you looking for?
He almost went
and said;

And are you looking
for a boy
that's fat, and nicely
fed?

But then he shut
his eyes, and thought
of other things
instead.

Jean Kenward

As I Looked Out

As I looked out on Saturday last,
A fat little pig went hurrying past.
Over his shoulders he wore a shawl,
Although it didn't seem cold at all.
I waved to him, but he didn't see,
For he never so much as looked at me.

Once again, when the moon was high,
I saw that pig come hurrying by.
Back he came at a terrible pace.
The moonlight shone on his little pink face,
And he smiled with a smile that was quite
    content.
But I never knew where that little pig went.

Anon

Are You Pleased with the Donkey You Bought at the Fair?

'Are you pleased with the donkey you bought
    at the fair?'
I asked the old man with the flowing white hair.
'Oh yes, a fine beast. I've had him since March.
But that bridge is a nuisance.
His ears catch on the arch.
So,
I'm cutting some grooves for his ears in the
    stone,
But it takes a long time
when you're working alone.'

'It's none of my business,' I said with a smile,
'But I had it in mind that it might be worth
    while
To dig out the path –
Less work don't you know.'

He thought for a minute and then answered
    slow,
'Ah, yes, but hold on, it's not how it appears;
He ain't long in the leg;
He's too long in the ears.'

Gregory Harrison

I Sat Belonely

I sat belonely down a tree,
humbled fat and small.
A little lady sing to me
I couldn't see at all.

I'm looking up and at the sky,
to find such wondrous voice.
Puzzly, puzzle, wonder why,
I hear but have no choice.

'Speak up, come forth, you ravel me,'
I potty menthol shout.
'I know you hiddy by this tree.'
But still she won't come out.

Such softly singing lulled me sleep,
an hour or two or so
I wakeny slow and took a peep
and still no lady show.

Then suddy on a little twig
I thought I see a sight,
A tiny little tiny pig,
that sing with all its might.

'I thought you were a lady,'
I giggle – well I may,
To my surprise the lady,
got up – and flew away.

John Lennon

The Porcupine

The porcupine is puzzled
that his friends should act so queer,
for though they come to visit him
they never come too near.

They often stop to say hello
and pass the time of day,
but still the closest of them all
stays many feet away.

He sits and ponders endlessly,
but never finds a clue
to why his close companions
act the distant way they do.

The porcupine has never had
the notion in his brain
that what he finds enjoyable
to others is a pain.

Jack Prelutsky

Riddle

A wee, wee house
Fou, fou o' meat,
Neither door nor window
To let you in to eat.

Egg

Just Think!

The Turkey

Turkeys don't like Christmas
which may come as no surprise.
They say why don't human beings
pick on people their own size.
To sit beside potatoes
in an oven can't be fun,
so a Turkey is quite justified
to feel he's being done.

Richard Digance

When I Grow Up

When I grow up I'd rather be
Anything other than boring old me –
A nurse, or a doctor, or maybe a VET.
I'll practice on the family pet.

Anon

Little Johnny

Little Johnny fished all day,
Fishes would not come his way.
'Had enough of this,' said he,
'I'll be going home to tea!'

When the fishes saw him go
Up they came all in a row;
Jumped about and laughed with glee,
Shouting, 'Johnny's gone to tea!'

Anon

The Sea

Behold the wonders of the mighty deep,
Where crabs and lobsters learn to creep,
And little fishes learn to swim,
And clumsy sailors tumble in.

Anon

Spot On

Imagination.
A fertile valley, nestling in a wilderness,
With a frog hopping about.
A spotted frog.

A spotted frog
Hopping, hoping it won't be seen,
Because a frog should never be seen by a . . .
Lesser spotted frog-eating bird.

I wander around,
Spotting spotted frogs,
And lesser spotted frog-eating-birds,
Spotting spotted frogs.

But lo!
There is a great lesser-spotted, spotted-frog-
    eating-
Bird,
Spotting spotted frogs as well.

On the horizon I can see a . . .
Small spotted, small little spotted small bird-
    eating
Frog spotter. Of course, he is spotting frogs.
Alas, alack, they are rare now.

Uncommon are the . . .
Small little spotted small bird-eating frogs.
But, of course, they don't eat . . .
Greater spotted frog-eating birds eating spotted
  frogs.

Such is imagination.
Incongruous.
Maybe the wilderness isn't so big.

I can see spots . . .

David Russell Watkins (aged 14)

Barney and Fred

Fancy eating your bed
Like the guinea pigs Barney and Fred
Who nibble away
Wood shavings and hay.

I should never feel
Like making my house a meal
And gnawing the wood
To do my teeth good.

I never met anyone yet
Who ate the floor and carpet
Except, as I said,
Barney and Fred.

Stanley Cook

Sparrow-Boys

These four birds are sparrow-boys
(Not barrow-boys
But sparrow-boys)
And they live in Peckham Rye.

These four birds are shady birds
(Not lady-birds
But shady birds)
They are what you might call sly.

These four birds are city birds
(Not pretty birds
But city birds)
And they really know what gives.

These four birds are shovey birds
(Not lovey birds
But shovey birds)
Four crafty slicked-up spivs!

Beware of these four sparrow-boys
(Not barrow-boys
But sparrow-boys)
When you're down in Peckham Rye.

For they're skin-you-in-a-minute birds
(Not linnet birds
But skinnit birds)
And there's nothing they won't try.

John Smith

Toucannery

Whatever one toucan can do
is sooner done by toucans.

Jack Prelutsky

Knock-kneed Chicken

I'm a knock-kneed chicken, I'm a bow-legged
    sparrow,
Missed my bus so I went by barrow.
I went to the café for my dinner and my tea,
Too many radishes – Hick! Pardon me.

Playground song

Animal Chatter

The other morning, feeling dog-tired, I was
   walking sluggishly to school,
When I happened upon two girls I know – who
   were busy playing the fool.
They were monkeying about, having a fight –
But all that they said didn't sound quite right.
'You're batty, you are – and you're catty too.'
'Don't be so waspish!' 'Don't be such a pig!'
'Look who's getting cocky – your head's too
   big!'
'You silly goose! Let me have my say!'
'Why should I, you elephantine popinjay?!'
I stopped, I looked, I listened – and I had to
   laugh
Because I realized then, of course, it's never the
   cow or the calf
That behave in this bovine way.
It's mulish humans like those girls I met the
   other day.
You may think I'm too dogged, but something
   fishy's going on –
The way we beastly people speak of animals is
   definitely wrong.
Crabs are rarely crabby and mice and never
   mousey
(And I believe all lice deny that they are lousy).
You know, if I wasn't so sheepish and if I had
   my way
I'd report the English language to the RSPCA.

Gyles Brandreth

P.S.

One That Got Away

Write a poem
About a lion they said,
So from memories
Of lions in my head
I wrote about
Tawny eyes and slashing claws,
Lashing tail and sabred jaws –
Didn't like what I had written
And began to cross it out –
Suddenly with a roar of rage
It sprang from the cage of lines
On the page
And rushed away into the blue,
A wounded lion poem
Half crossed through!
It's one that got away
Haven't seen it to this day
But I carefully look,
In case it's crouching, growling,
Licking its wounds and waiting,
Under cover in the leaves
Inside some other book.

And here I sit
After all this time,
Still not having written
A poem about a lion.

Julie Holder

Index of Titles

Index of Authors

Acknowledgements

The editors and publishers wish to thank the following for giving permission to include in this anthology material which is their copyright. All efforts have been made to contact copyright holders. If we have inadvertently omitted to acknowledge anyone, we should be most grateful if this could be brought to our attention for correction at the first opportunity.

B T Batsford Limited for 'The Hen' by John Joy Bell from *The Children's Book of Comic Verse*.

Captain Beaky Limited for 'Norman the Zebra' and 'Cyril the Centipede' by Jeremy Lloyd from the *Captain Beaky Book Volume 1* by Chappell Music Limited (1976). Trademark Captain Beaky T.M.

Adam and Charles Black Publishers for 'Snowblind' by Geoffrey Summerfield from *Bric-a-Brac* ed. Peggy Blakely.

Cadbury Limited for 'Pigs' by Katie Sandford and 'The Eccentric Elephant' by Helen Boddy from *Cadbury's Second Book of Children's Poetry*, and 'Spot On' by David Russell Watkins from *Cadbury's First Book of Children's Poetry*.

Gyles Brandreth for 'Animal Chatter' from *A Fourth Poetry Book* ed. OUP. Burke Publishing Company Limited for 'Sparrow Boys' by John Smith from *The Early Bird and the Worm*.

Jonathan Cape Limited for 'The Infant Elephant Speaks' by Adrian Mitchell from *The Apeman Cometh*; and 'I Sat Belonely' by John Lennon from *In His Own Write*. (We also acknowledge The Estate of John Lennon.)

Edward Coleman for the Lord Alfred Douglas Literary Estate for 'The Lion', 'The Weasel' and 'The Ferret' by Lord Alfred Douglas from *The Batsford Book of Light Verse for Children*.

Stanley Cook for 'Barney and Fred' from *Come Along: Poems for Younger Children* pub. by the author.

J M Dent and Sons Limited for 'House Flies' by N M Bodecker from *Hurry, Hurry Mary Dear*.

André Deutsch for 'Christmas Dinner' by Michael Rosen from *Quick, Let's Get Out of Here*.

Dobson Books Limited for 'The Duck Billed Platypus' and 'The Walrus' by Michael Flanders/Marcello Minale from *Creatures Great and Small*.

Duckworth and Company Limited for 'The Yak' and 'The Elephant' by Hilaire Belloc from *Complete Verse*.

Faber and Faber Publishers for 'The Geese in Greece' by N M Bodecker from *Let's Marry Said The Cherry*; 'The Whale' and 'The Sloth' by Theodore Roethke from *The Collected Poems of Theodore Roethke*; 'My Grandpa' by Ted Hughes from *Meet My Folks*.

Fontana Paperbacks for 'Sergeant Brown's Parrot' by Kit Wright from *Rabbiting On*.

Gregory Harrison: 'Are You Pleased With The Donkey?' from *A Third Poetry Book* pub OUP Copyright © reprinted by permission of the author.

William Heineman Limited for 'The Frog's Lament' by Aileen Fisher from *In the Woods, In the Meadow, In the Sky*; 'The Hairy Dog' by Herbert Asquith and 'The Nonny' and 'The Bogus-Boo' by James Reeves from *Pillicock Hill, Prefabulous Animiles and More Prefabulous Animiles*.